My Picture Tells A Story

Cover designed by Neal Schlosburg

Neal Schlosburg
Visit my website at www.mypicturetellsastory.com

Printed in the United States of America

First Printing: March 2020

ISBN-978-0-578-63676-4

In loving memory of Jim Auerbach.
Friend, mentor, and fellow photographer.

ACKNOWLEDGEMENTS

Gail Weiss, a wonderful, kind, loving woman who I am thankful to have as my dear friend, inspiration, sounding board, and objective curator of my art. As Gail's close friend, I am fortunate and joyful, to have her in my life.

Billy, Tim, Skyla, Erinn, Fekadu, Johanna, Lisa, Shanae, Amanda M., Heather, Brian, Allen, Cristina, Jenny, Sue, Connie, Beverly, Jeremy, Amanda S., and Robin, my story tellers and twenty of the most amazing, caring, courageous people an artist could ever hope to work with. They are my family and I am eternally grateful to each of them.

Jimi Giannatti, photographer extraordinaire and author of the Forward for this book. Soulmate, brother, fellow music lover, Jimi's portrait work is an inspiration. His photos that now hang in the permanent collection of the UCLA African American Library were particularly impactful on my own portrait work. Jimi's photographs were on the cover of Spin Magazine, among others. He's photographed Will Smith, Cindy Crawford, Jamie Foxx, John Wooden, Muhammad Ali, and more. I am grateful for his kind words that open this book.

Mallory Heinrich and Johanna Cruz, lead editor and associate editor respectively. They are two incredibly talented women. Somehow these two make my words coherent and pithy. Pithy is a word my son Avi introduced me to many years ago. Mallory and Johanna take my attempts at being pithy and make them pithier.

Michael Austin Stevens, my cousin Bunny, and Patty Hankins, important touchstones in the history of *My Picture Tells A Story.*

Jeff "SpryTime" Miller, Aurore Rominger, and Jimi Giannatti, my sounding board and book review committee. Three fellow photographers and artists whose friendship I cherish. Their craft and art inspire me.

Dona Jones and Judith Olivia HeartSong, amazing artists and very accomplished women, their friendship and support opened the doors that made this project possible.

Jim Auerbach, longtime friend, brilliant travel photographer, the man whose insistent but gentle pushes helped me get out of my own way. He was Gandalf to my Bilbo, pushing me out my door and into an adventure that eventually led me here.

Kathy Klenner, Meg Copas, and Kelly Barry, three special colleagues and dear friends from Payroll Network. Their encouragement and support throughout my photo art endeavors was something I never experienced in a work environment, especially from senior management. They each played an important role, notably as I got the opportunities to start exhibiting.

My Payroll Network Family, an incredible group of people I can honestly say are more family than work colleagues. Payroll Network is a nurturing and caring company I've called home for over thirteen years. The best thirteen plus years of my life. Built by Charlie Wolf, it's a company that truly cares about the people who work for him. As an artist, I could not have been in a better place as I pursued my lifelong dreams, especially in the last five years.

Artist and Makers and the Artist and Markers' Artist Community, a place built by an artist, for artists, in support of artists. Judith Olivia HeartSong, executive director and incredible artist in her own right, and all the artists in this wonderful community comprise a space where artists create, thrive, support, and nurture each other. It is my artistic home.

Julius Schlosburg, brilliant Tucson photographer, Julius is the photographer for my bio photo. I am grateful to be the father of this beautiful young man.

To my twenty story tellers.
Without their courage, *My Picture Tells A Story* was not possible.

CONTENTS

Just like children, emotions heal when they are heard and validated.

—JILL BOLTE TAYLOR, *MY STROKE OF INSIGHT: A BRAIN SCIENTIST'S PERSONAL JOURNEY*

My Picture Tells A Story

twenty stories by twenty people
a unique portrait study in human emotions

Neal Schlosburg

FORWARD

"There are always two people in every picture: the photographer and the viewer." -- Ansel Adams
"The quickest way to make money at photography is to sell your camera." -- Anonymous

It's an odd thing when you decide to make a career out of what is a hobby for most. For the pro photographers I have known and worked with over the past forty-five years, being a professional photographer seems to have been less a conscious decision, and more of a "calling". I've come to believe that you can't teach a person to become a "true" photographer, as much as encourage their inner photographer within them to come out. You can teach a person the mechanics of the camera and how light works; but you can't teach him that certain *je ne sais quoi* that makes a person a pro. Today, with millions of photos being posted to social media sites all over the world by non-professionals, being a professional photographer is more challenging than ever. What distinguishes the "professional" over the array of amateurs armed with their cell phone and Instagram portfolios anyway?

In 2014, according to Mary Meeker's annual Internet Trends report, people uploaded an average of 1.8 billion digital images every single day. That's 657 billion photos per year. Another way to think about it is that for every two minutes, humans take more photos than ever existed in total 150 years ago. Some of these photos are quite exceptional; worthy of being in any professional photographer's portfolio. But in my mind, that doesn't make any of them actual photographers, but rather people just taking pictures.

Like tourists traveling through their own lives, amateurs mostly photograph what is directly in front of them. They have their subject stand in front of the Eiffel Tower and they "snap!" - stand in front of the Grand Canyon and they "click!" Sunsets, rainbows, dogs, kids, chance encounters with celebrities, a beautiful vista, and salads seem to be the predominant subject matter that make up the portfolios of the amateurs that permeates our social media feeds. In contrast, whereas an amateur will shoot what's directly in front of them, a pro conjures their photos. They craft their photograph like an architect. A professional will often already have a rough idea of what they want to shoot before they even pick up their camera.

Professionals have a story to tell with their images. It's rare that any of their work is created from a vacuum. Ansel Adams, Dorothea Lange, Richard Avedon, Mary Ellen Mark, and so many more, all leave an indelible personal stamp of themselves within each photograph they create. Having this ability to capture an image that comes from their heart, as much as it does from their mind, is a gift. My dear friend Neal Schlosburg has this gift.

I first met Neal "in person" years ago in a small bar named PLUSH located in downtown Tucson, where his son, Julius, was playing drums with a local band. But I had many conversations with him previously online in the virtual world. I had been hired to photograph his son's band's promotional photos, and Julius (an amazing photographer in his own right) told me that his father was also a photographer. After posting some of the band's photos on social media, Neal messaged me and introduced himself. We struck up an instant friendship; discussing everything from politics to coffee; but mostly we talked about photography. By the time I finally met Neal in person, he and I already felt as if we'd been friends for a while. Neal's unbridled enthusiasm and passion about photography always came through in our online conversations, but in person, his love of taking photographs radiated from him. He simply got it. I knew then, he was the real deal.

I can recall a conversation we had on a train early on the morning of March 24, in 2018, as we were both headed to Washington, DC to photograph The March for Our Lives demonstration that supported legislation to prevent gun violence in the United States. He was "riffing" about a different way he wanted to photograph the participants of the march. No matter what, capturing the raw emotion of the young student demonstrators was paramount in his intent.

As we made our way through the nearly 800,000 people who showed up that day, we both strategized as where we should be to get what we came for. I decided to roam and seek out the different groups and capture them within the iconic background of Washington, DC. Neal decided on a completely different take. He found a spot, dropped down on one knee, then turned towards the marchers and photographed them as they walked towards him. This unorthodox angle gave special meaning to the march's participants. Shooting from the low angle gave them a heroic "real-life" quality. Afterwards, while showing me some of his edited shots of that day, he became emotional recalling the impact that the event had on him. This is why I say Neal is a "true" photographer; he is as much a part of the photo as the subjects are. The work Neal creates is as much for himself, as it is for his subjects and us viewers.

The portraits on the following pages of this book underscores this symbiotic relationship Neal has with his art. The unique choices he makes in the editing of his images jumps out at you! The viewer feels the spontaneity. Everything we see in each portrait has been produced with intense deliberation. Art, as I stated before, doesn't happen in a vacuum. As you look at the photos please keep in mind, just as in a beautiful dance, the sequences he pieces together in each portrait first "came to life" by Neal and his story tellers in the studio. Later, they were stitched together during post-production; editing them to produce a wide range of emotions and compositions that Neal saw in each person as their stories unfolded. When you view each portrait, you are actually seeing two portraits: the subject's and the photographer's.

Please enjoy this collection of work created by Neal Schlosburg.

Jimi Giannatti

PREFACE

The Motivation - Sharing emotions and troubling stories with family members or close friends is difficult for many people. We are afraid of what others will think of us. Society tells us not to burden others with our troubles.

Instead, many of us internalize them, blow them off when we need to share them, even tell them to an inappropriate person. It affects our moods, our outlook, our day to day life, and our relationships. Some swear they will take these feelings and stories to their grave. Unfortunately, some do sooner than later.

People tell me their personal stories and I listen to them without judgment. In telling their stories, I use unique images. My work shows that sharing personal and emotional stories can be safe. Yours can be too.

The Project was twenty volunteers, telling twenty stories, on twenty separate prints, with six images on each print. Each tells a complete story.

Over a period of 26 months, Billy, Tim, Skyla, Erinn, Fekadu, Johanna, Lisa, Shanae, Amanda M., Heather, Brian, Allen, Cristina, Jenny, Sue, Connie, Beverly, Jeremy, Amanda S., and Robin each told me their very personal story. For the story sessions, each dressed, sat, spoke, and moved as they chose. They were never rehearsed, prompted, or interrupted. I never spoke. Each story took 7 to 90 minutes to tell. For each story, I took 150 to 1,500 images. From those images, I chose 6 images in chronological order to tell you their story.

I am eternally grateful to each one for their trust in me, and their support and love in this endeavor. None of this is possible without their willingness to bring "My Picture Tells A Story" to life.

The Musical Connection - Music has been an essential part of my life, and it entered the creative process in an unexpected way. Looking at one of my fine art images, a large delicate white flower with linen like petals, Gail, my close companion, said it reminded her of a beautiful wedding dress. The moment she made that comment, Billy Idol's "White Wedding" played in my head. Since then, all my images are named after a song title, an album title, or a band name.

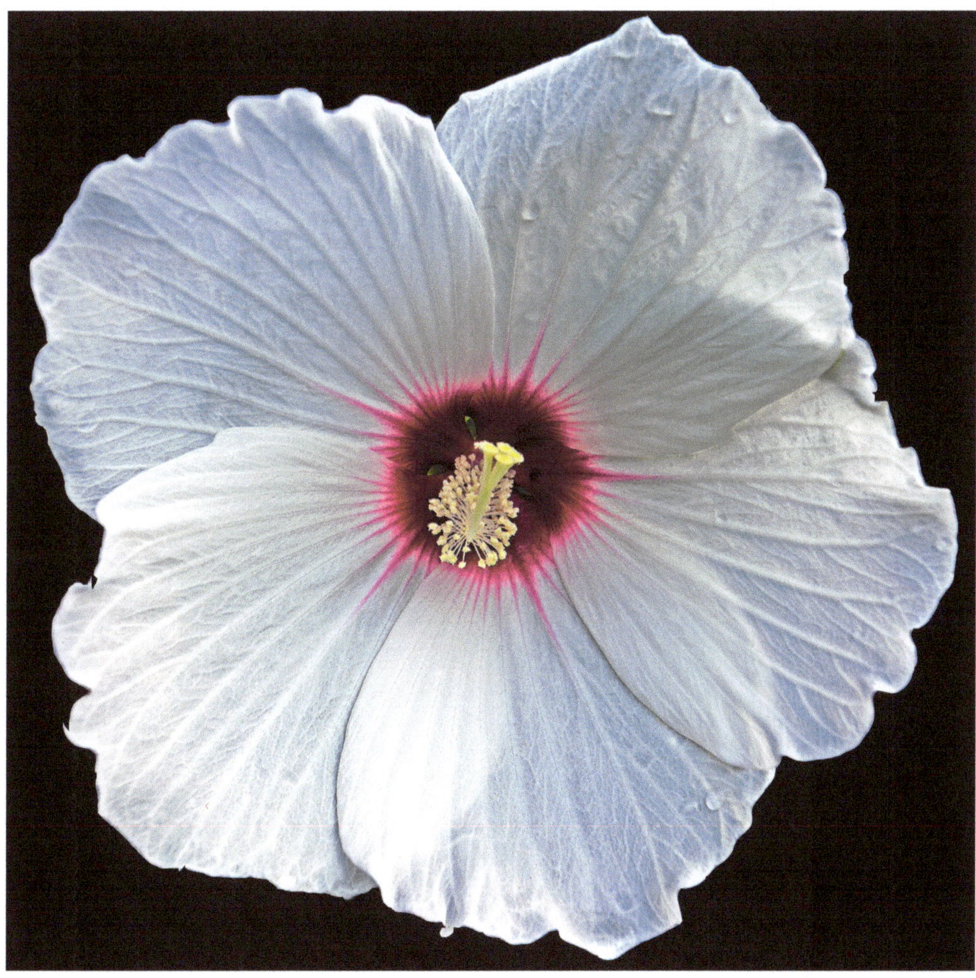

THE STORY BEHIND THE STORIES

CAN WE TAKE ANOTHER PICTURE?

THE HISTORY

The Genesis – July 25, 2015

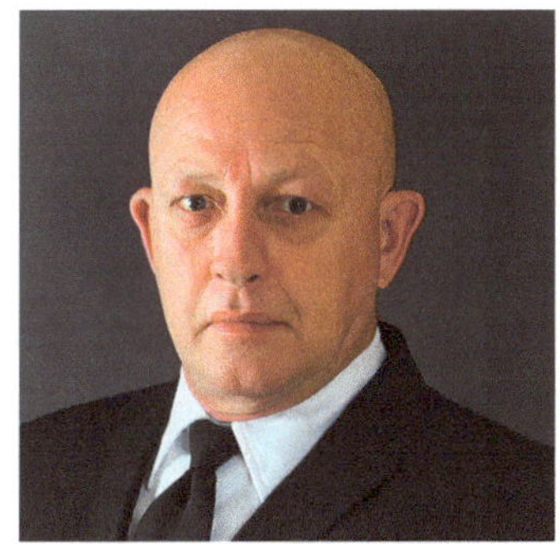

Michael Austin Stevens

Mr. Stevens, who used his middle name, at least with me, contacted me to photograph his business headshot for LinkedIn and other social media. At the time, Austin was a lifelong Military transitioning into the Civilian work world.

The photo session was very straight forward. Austin knew what he wanted, and the session was completed within 10 minutes of the first pose. During Austin's time on the posing stool, he was able to see his image right after I took each shot. I have a large monitor in my studio. Not only do I see the images right after each shot; so do my clients. After a few shots, Austin and I agreed we had the right image.

After each session ends, the client pays for the service by check or credit. If not for a quirk of faith would the image that became the genesis for *My Picture Tells A Story* be taken.

Me: "Austin, would like to use check or credit card?"

Austin: "How about cash?" "No one ever gives me cash, Austin." I replied. "Well, you'll take it won't you?" Austin asked. "Of course." I responded.

He gives me too much money and... "Austin, this is too much money. I don't have change for this. No one ever gives me cash." I said. "Can we take another picture?" Austin asked. It was less than what I'd usually charge for a second image but... Sure! Let's go back into the studio. I responded.

I asked Austin to take off his coat and tie for a more casual look. The first 2 shots were not to my liking. I decided to do something very different... something I've never done in a portrait session before.

Standing in front of him, I asked him to put his coat back on. Then I asked him that whatever was in his head, whatever he was feeling right then, go there. I asked him to wait a moment until I turned around and walked back to my camera. When I got to the camera, I said I'd turn around and press the shutter release immediately. That image came up on the studio monitor. We both thought it looked interesting and decided to stop there.

The Picture

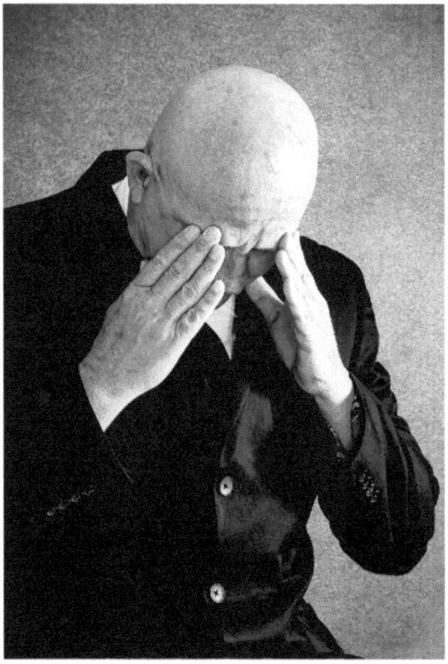

One day later, I started the post photo session work in Photoshop. The business shot of Austin was a straightforward, classic business image. The second shot was a very different story. I stared at it for 15 minutes. In front of me was an image that as a business portrait photographer, I had not photographed before. It was a spontaneous, emotional response for me to capture in a portrait setting. Long ago, my beginning days as an artist were using charcoal and pastels, not a camera. I let the emotion of the image carry my artistic instincts.

Along with a note, I sent the finished images to Austin. In the note, I mentioned that I had never finished an image the way I did with his second portrait. I also let him know that if he did not like the way I did it, I'd do it over.

His response was "Don't you dare touch it."

Responses

Including the back story, I posted the image on a photography Facebook page. I was expecting feedback on the quality and technical side of Austin's picture, but that didn't happen. Instead, I got a string of personal comments. Some by people that were in the same situation, had been in that situation, or were close to someone going through it.

I continued to receive emotional responses to Austin's image and the story it told. Before I showed the image to someone, I always told the story behind it. The story was simple, "This is Austin. He's a lifelong Military transitioning into the Civilian world." The most compelling reaction came from an acquaintance and fellow photographer. I didn't know he was ex-Military prior to showing him the image. When Dan saw the image, his response was emphatic. "I know exactly how he feels. That was me."

Although I continued the business portraits, I soon started doing street photography, but the desire to photograph spontaneous human emotion in a portrait setting stayed with me. It would become a driving passion to create human images that people could form an emotional connection with.

The Technique – March 19, 2017

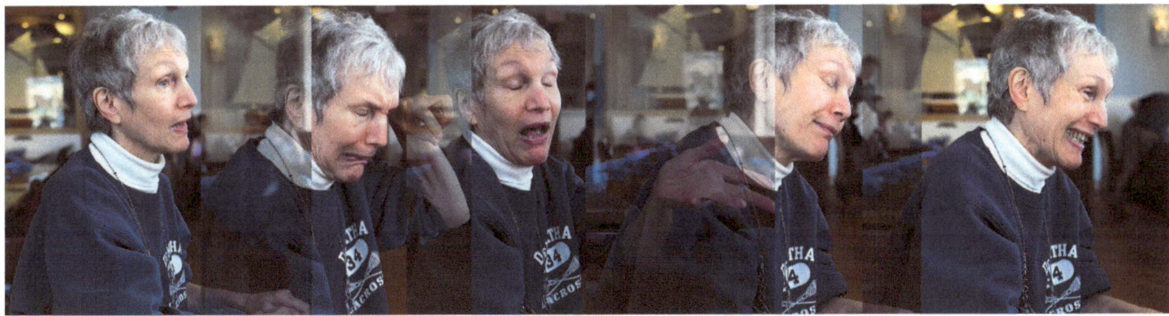

That Sunday morning, I went to a cousin's brunch. I happened to be testing a new lens that weekend and brought it with me. I might use it to compliment my other lenses for street photography in the future. It's also a great lens for sitting at a table and capturing inmate images of people up close without being intrusive.

I was photographing randomly throughout when I noticed my cousin Bunny starting to tell a story. She was telling it to a few cousins across and slightly to the right of me. Bunny was seated directly across from me. She is very animated when she talks, especially when she is relaying a tale. I started shooting and captured about a dozen images. The thought was that I would have one or two images out of this group that I really liked. When I put the images up on my editing viewer, my reaction was something entirely different. What I saw was an old-time film strip or story board. What would it look like if I took five of the images and put them together on a single canvas or print? I let my creative instincts take over; I created a complete story on a single print using multiple images.

Over a period of time, I showed the print to a few fellow photographers. Their responses were positive and encouraging.

LensWork and the Seeing in Sixes Project – April to June 2017

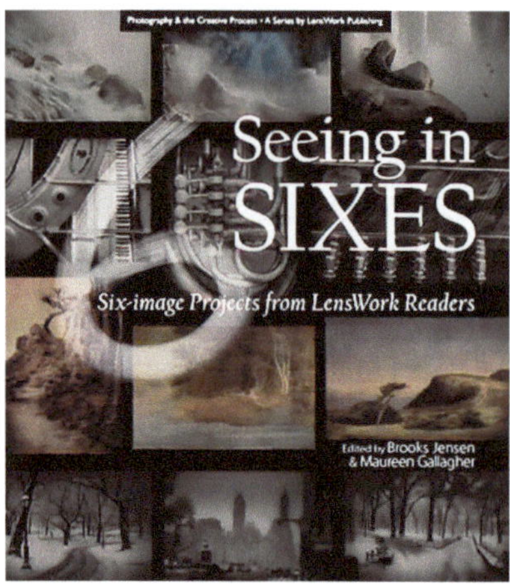

In 2016, LensWork Magazine introduced the Seeing in Sixes project. The concept was simple: create six separate interrelated images. The idea was to stimulate photographers by using this concept. It was a way to jump start the creative process. They would publish the 50 best projects they received. The submissions were worldwide. Several of my colleagues used the concept simply to start their own projects. A few submitted theirs for consideration. The publication is annual with the last one in 2019.

The Challenge – July 2017

I met with Patty Hankins, a fellow photographer to discuss my first solo exhibit set to open in October 2018. We discussed much, but the one thing she emphasized was a centerpiece or anchor for the exhibit. The exhibit was titled *The Color in Black & White*, an exhibit of only black and white images. Towards the end of our discussion, Patty challenged me to do a Seeing in Sixes project, maybe something that might end up in the exhibit. Since I was familiar with the concept of Seeing in Sixes, I found it intriguing, if not thought provoking.

The First Six – October 4th, 2017

Towards the end of September, I was struck with an idea that would later turn out to be the centerpiece for the upcoming exhibit and go on to become *My Picture Tells A Story*. What if I had six people tell me their story, using six images on each canvas? Six people, telling six stories, with six images on six prints; the ideal Seeing in Sixes project.

The Email

Once the concept was born, I needed six volunteers. I decided to take a chance and seek out volunteers where I work (my day job). That October was my eleventh year at the wonderful and supportive company, Payroll Network.

I sent an email to all my fellows at Payroll Network:

Subject: 6 Volunteers for a Photography Project

I am looking for 6 volunteers to help with a photography project I am undertaking.

It will take maybe 10 to 15 minutes to complete this with each volunteer. The photographs would be shot during a lunch break, before work, or after work.... your choice.

I am only looking to do one volunteer on any given day.

What it entails is this:

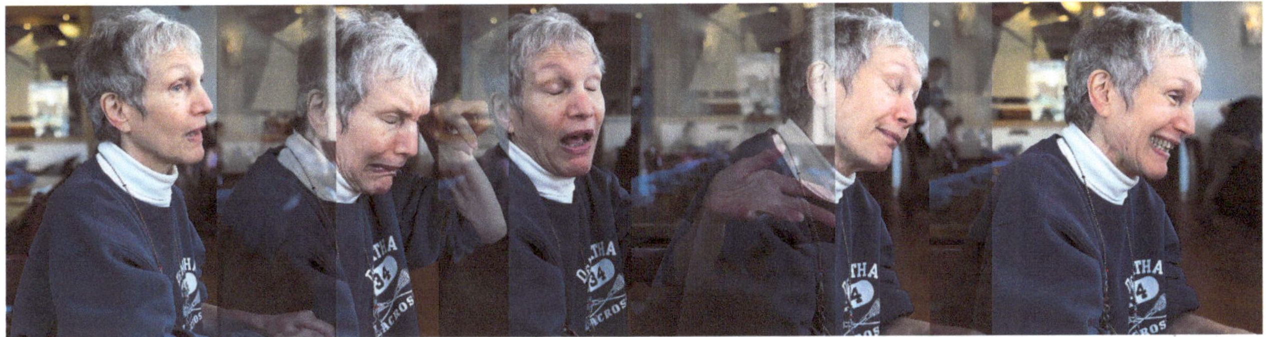

The finished photo strip will be in black & white and will be 6 shots instead of the 5 you see above.

The finished photo strips will be part of my first solo exhibit that will be in October 2018 at the Artist & Makers II Gallery in Rockville. All the photographs that will be exhibited will be in black & white – The Exhibit Is Titled *The Color in Black & White.*

Please don't hesitate to talk with me before you volunteer if you need more info.

This should be a lot fun for those that do volunteer. 😊

I received more than six volunteers. I took the first six: Johanna, Skyla, Erinn, Bill, Fekadu, and Tim. *My Picture Tells A Story* came to life.

THE STORIES

BILLY

Boulevard Of Broken Dreams

Divorce

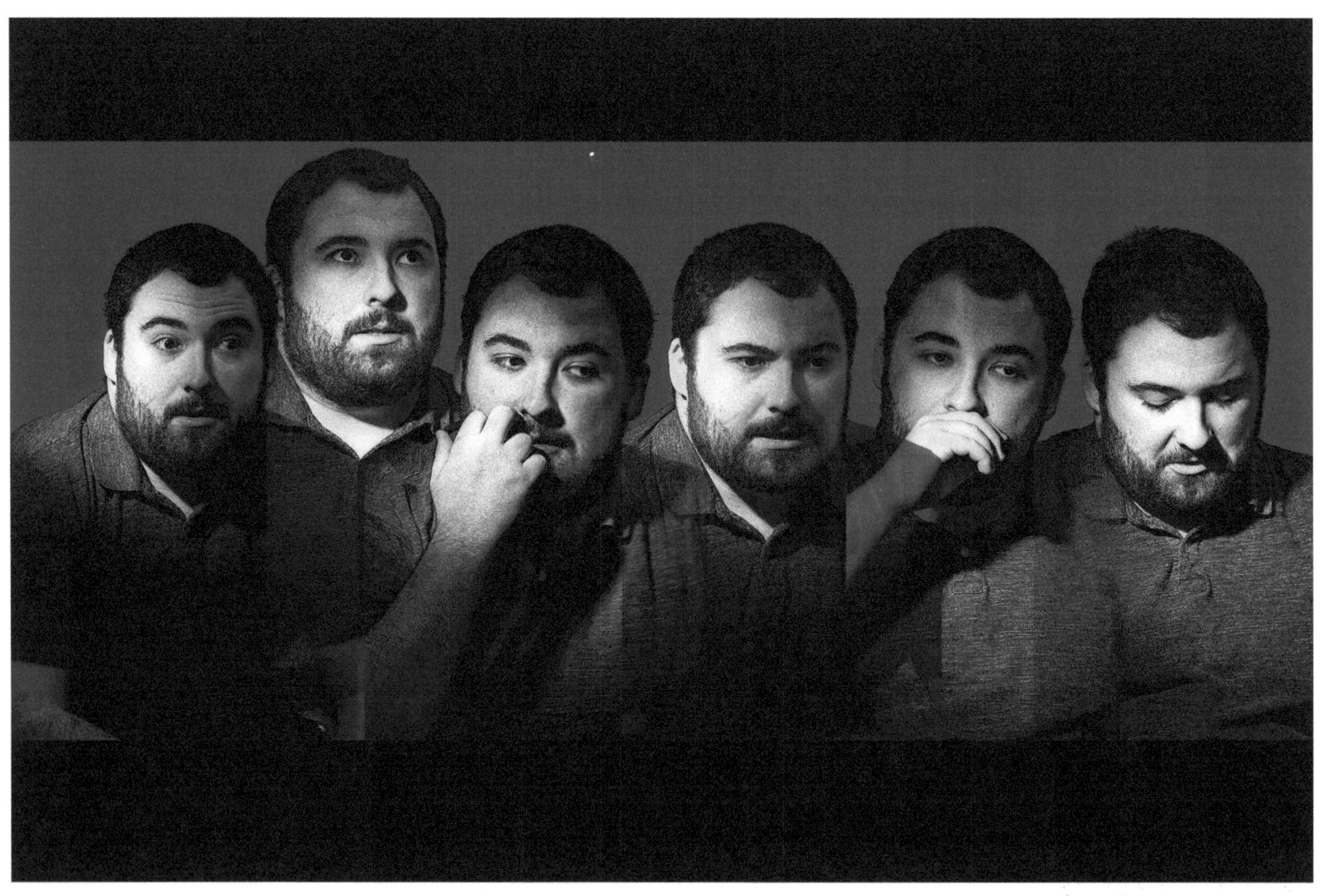

Story told on Thursday, November 9, 2017 — Title - Green Day

FEKADU

The Long And Winding Road

Missing His Homeland

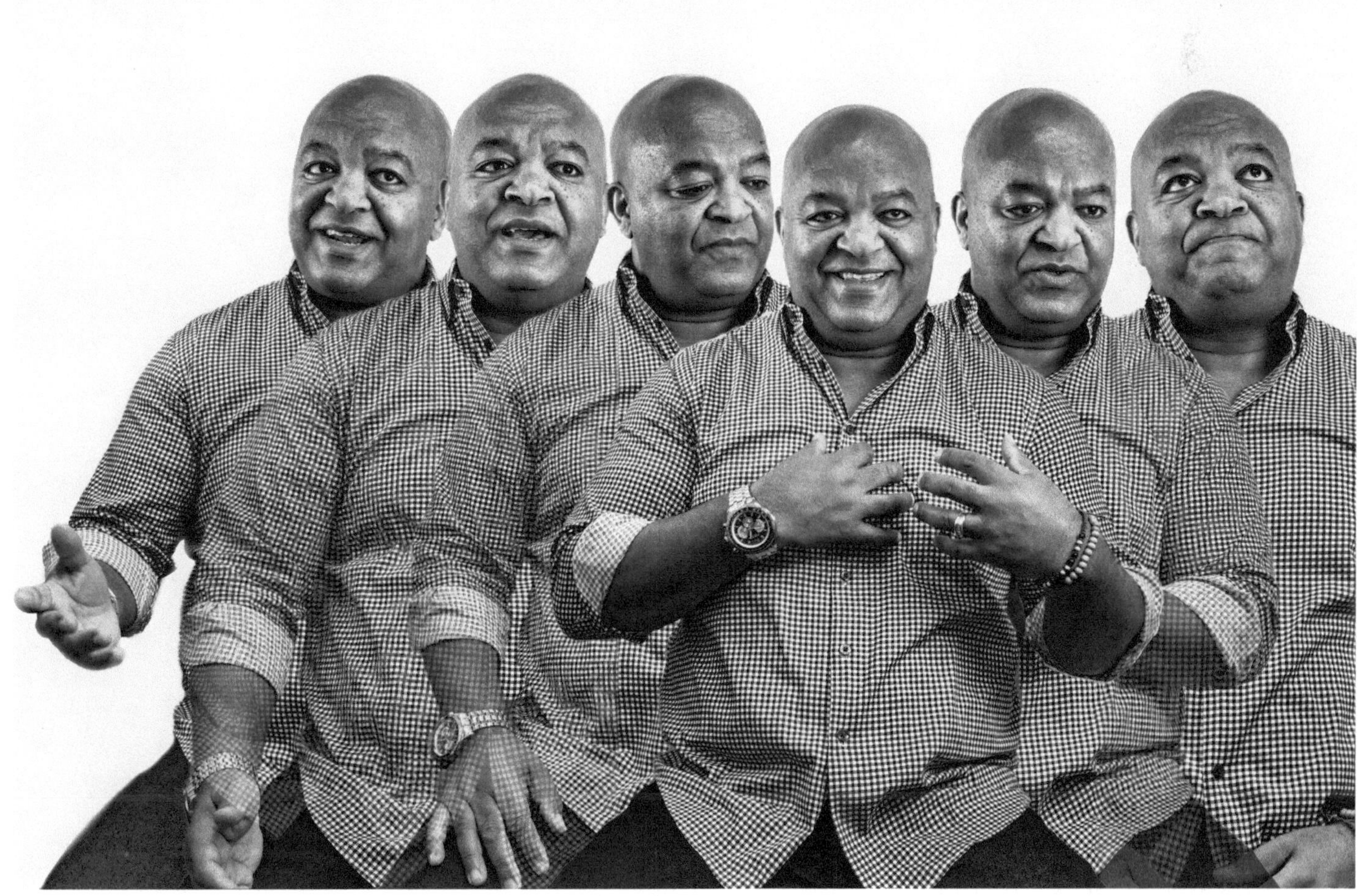

Story told on Thursday, June 28, 2018 — Title – Lennon – McCartney

SKYLA

(I Can't Get No) Satisfaction

Body Image

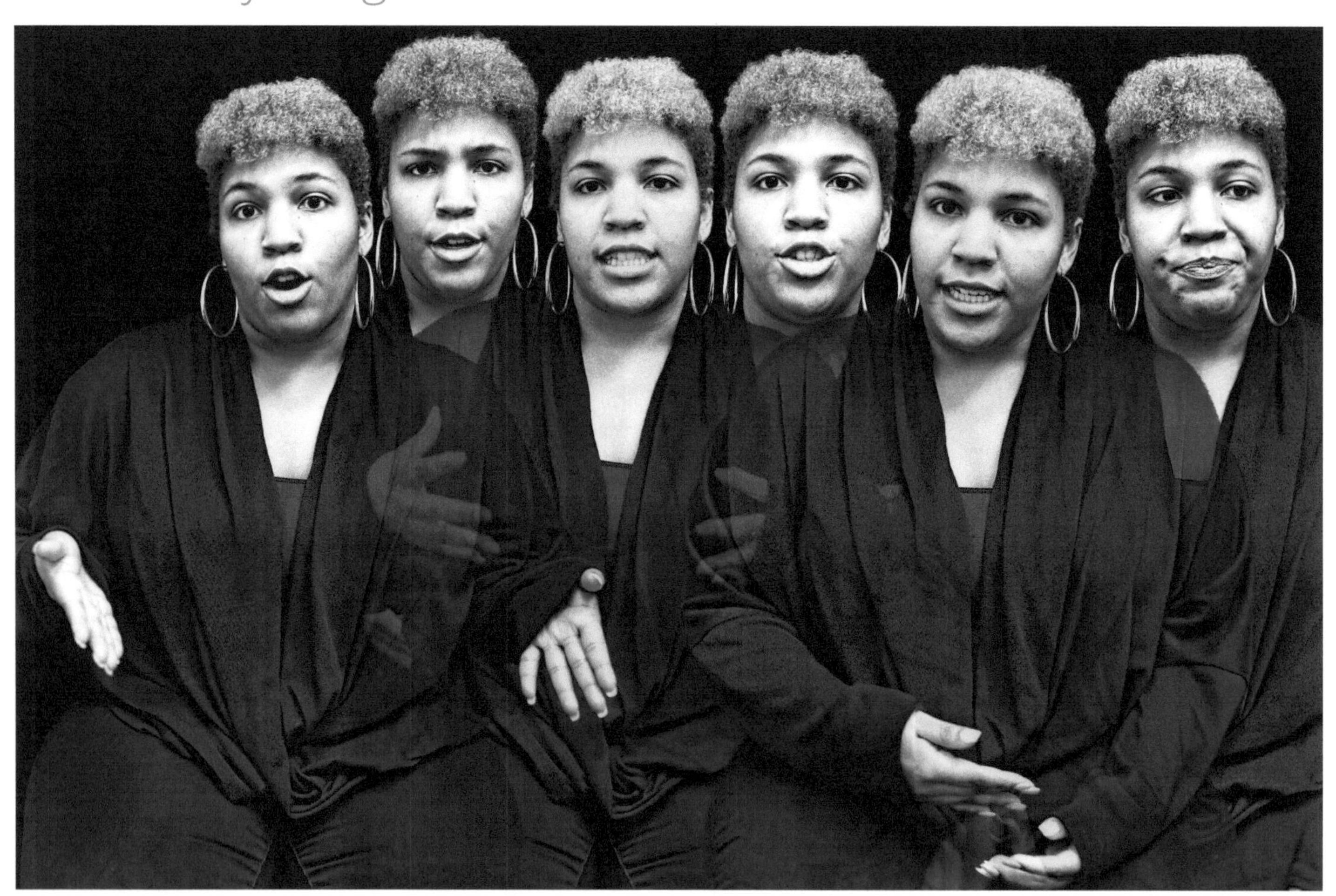

Story told on Friday, April 20, 2018 Title - Mick Jagger & Keith Richards

LISA

In My Life

Family Memories, Disney

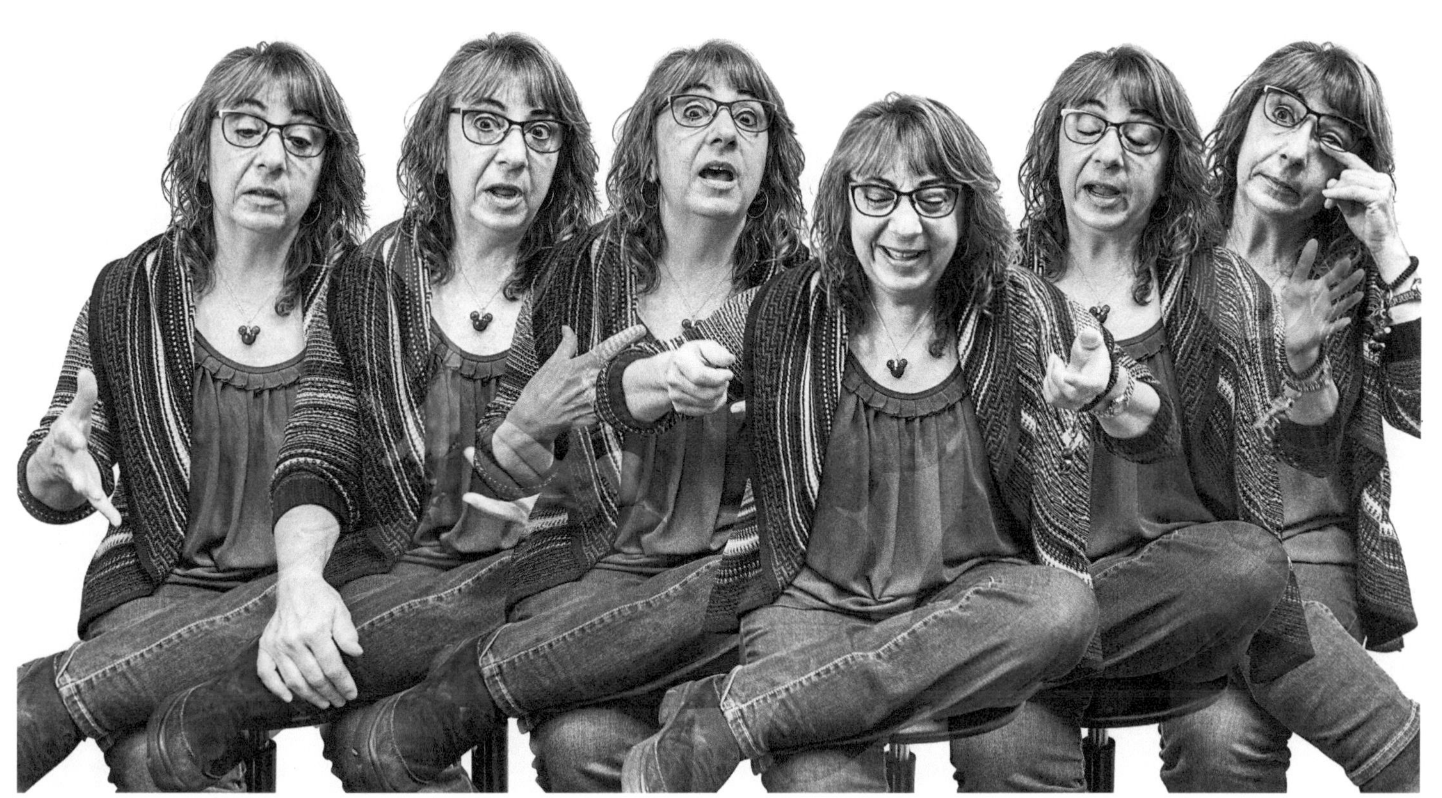

Story told on Thursday, January 31, 2019 Title - Lennon – McCartney

CRISTINA

Let It Be

The Road to Gratitude and Grace

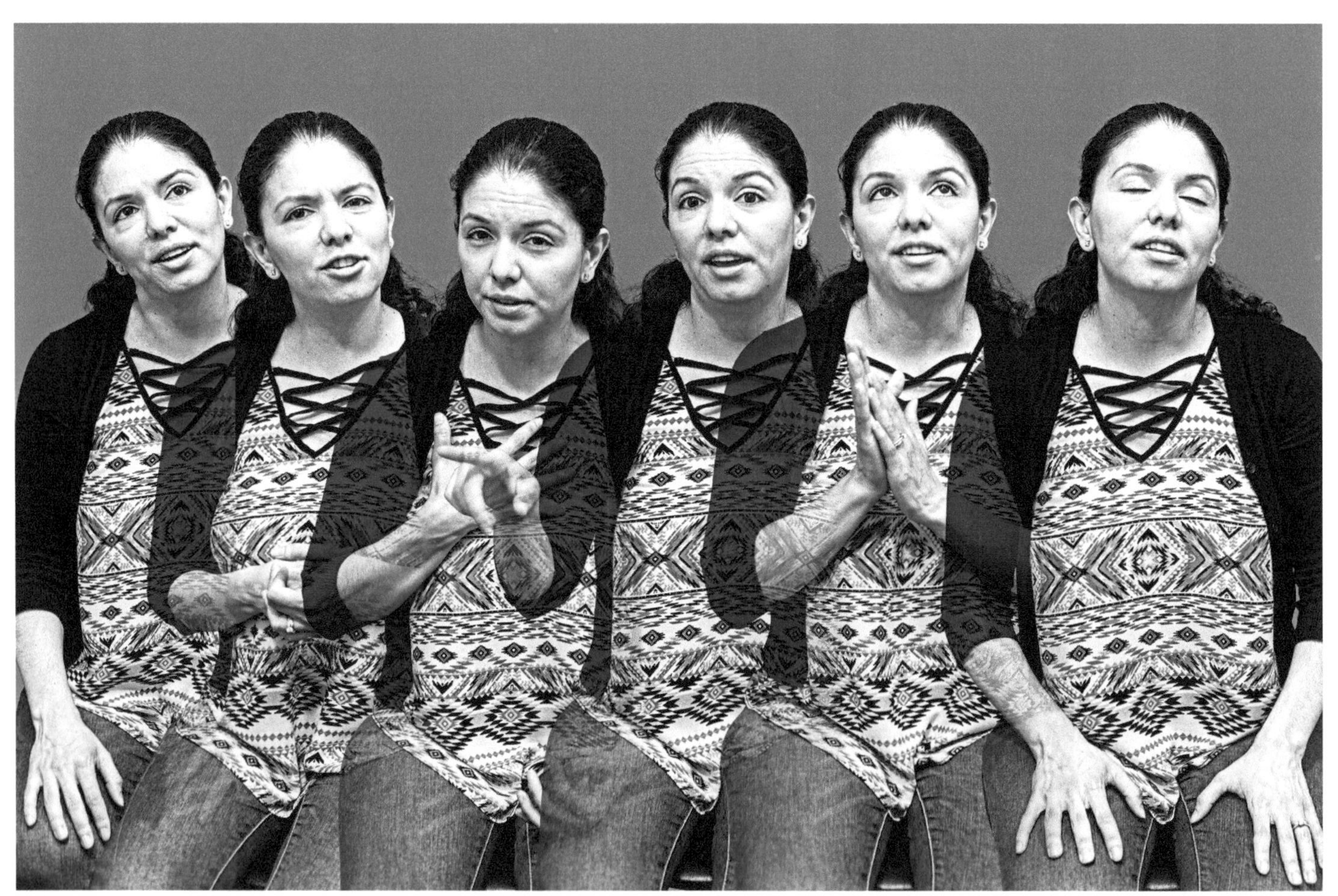

Story told on Friday, July 19, 2019 — Title - Lennon – McCartney

ROBIN

Grandma's Garden

A Grandmother's Love, Lessons, and Blessings

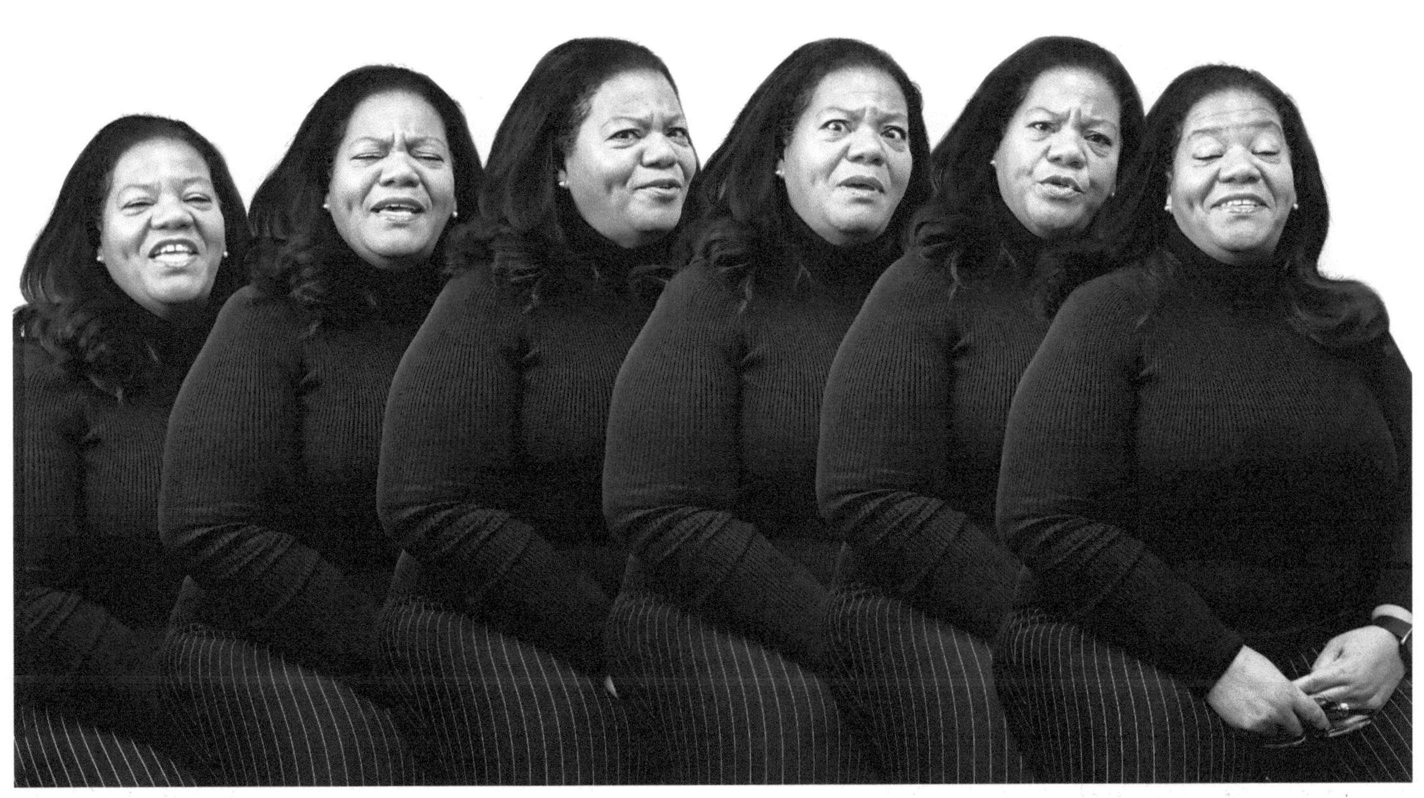

Story told on Friday, December 27, 2019

Title - Zac Brown

JOHANNA

I Won't Back Down

Health and Motivation

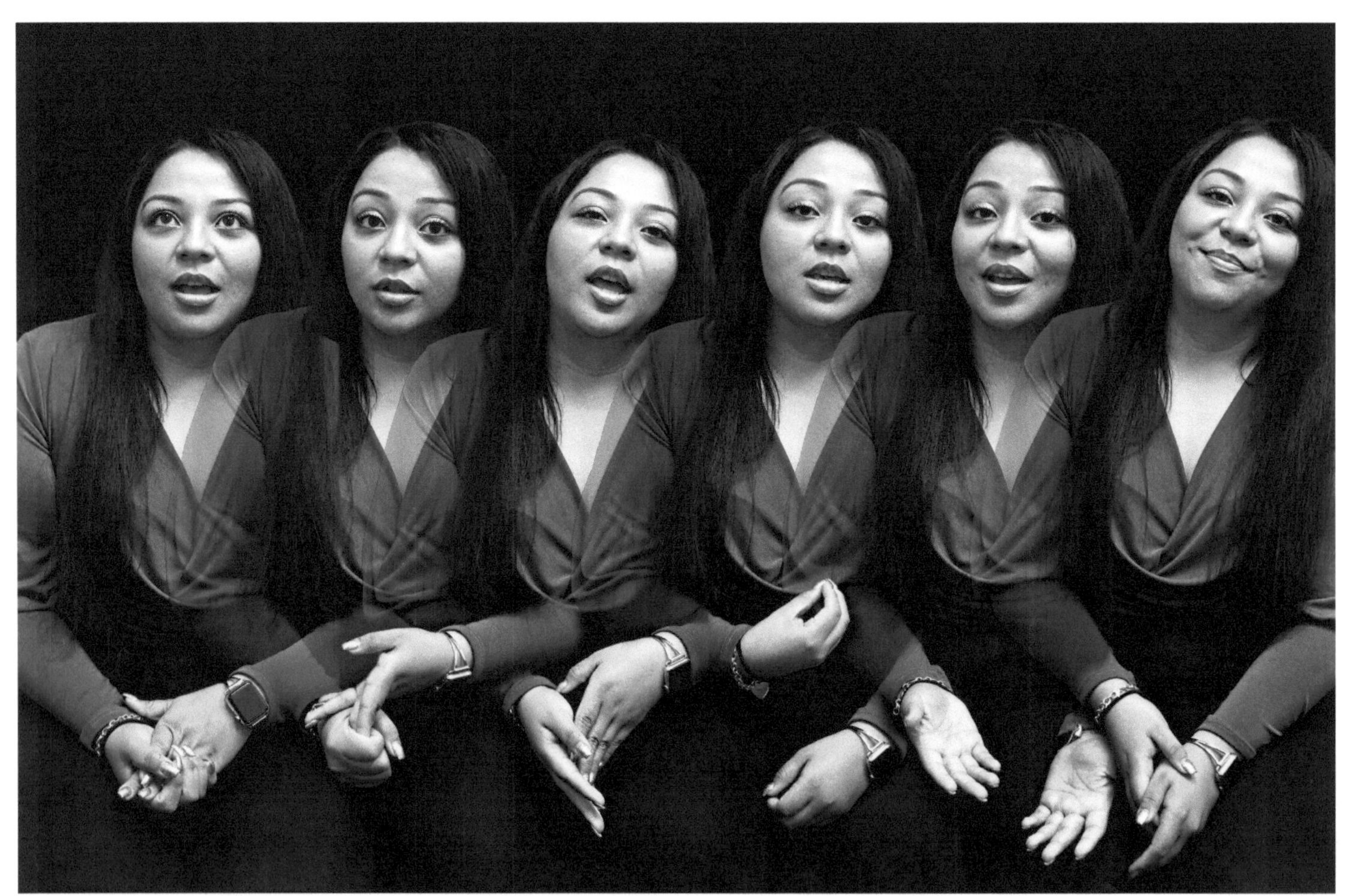

Story told on Friday, July 27, 2018 | Title - Tom Petty & Jeff Lynne

BRIAN

Calm Inside The Storm

Facing Disaster, Surviving Two Crashes

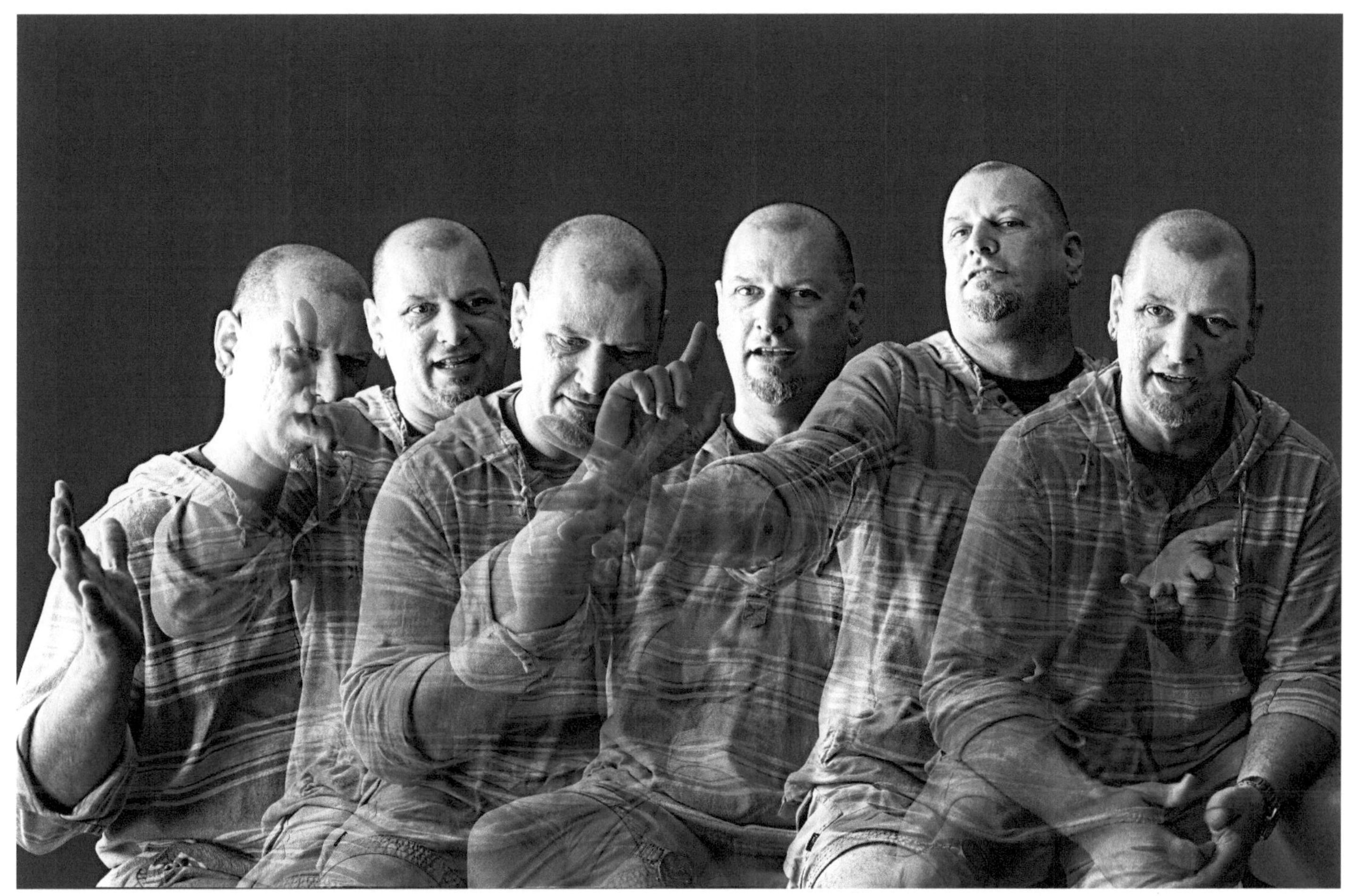

Story told on Saturday, May 18, 2019 | Title - Cyndi Lauper

SHANAE

You Don't Know Me

Self-love

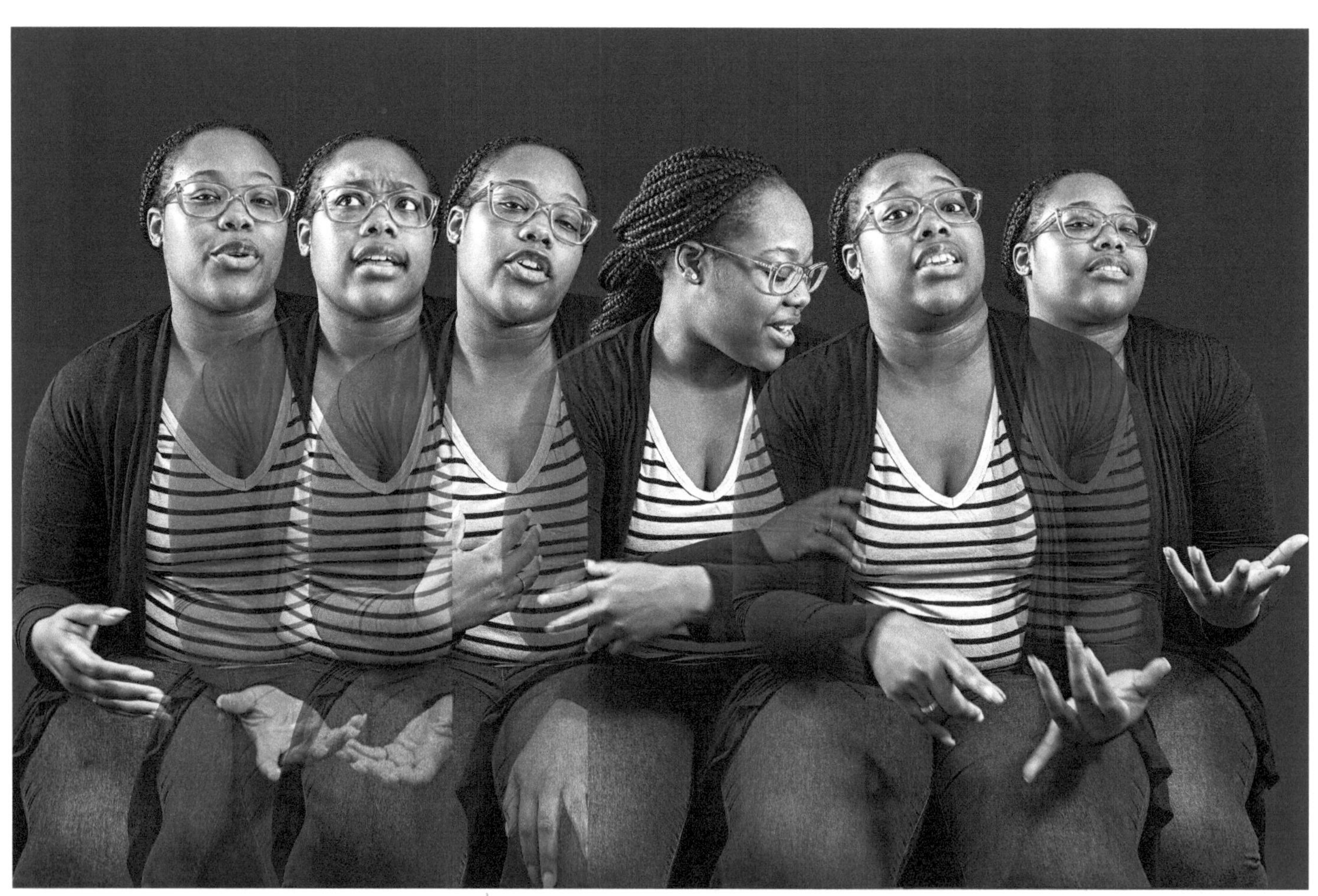

Story told on Friday, February 8, 2019 Title - Ray Charles

ALLEN

I Can't Hide From My Mind

Masking Reality

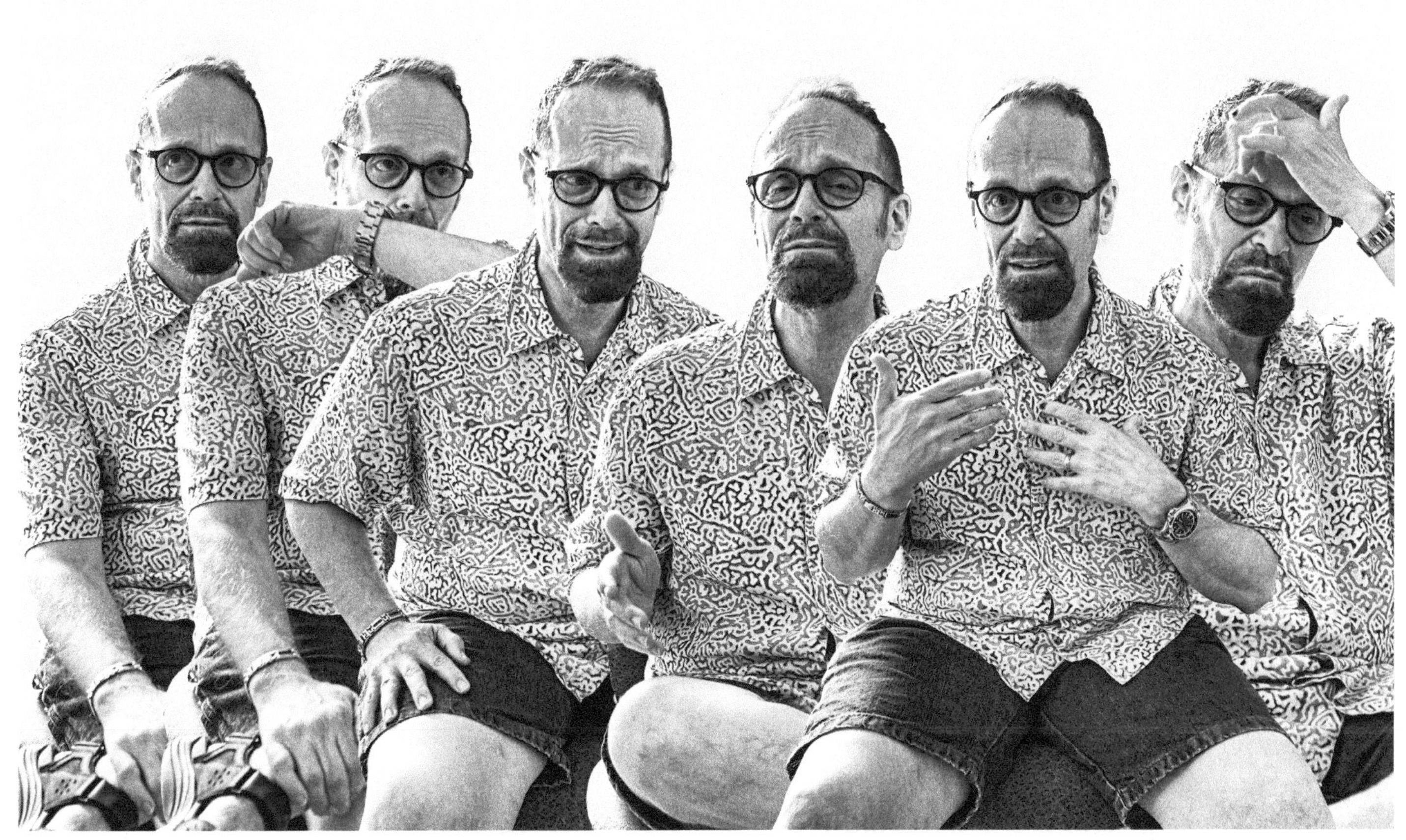

Story told on Saturday, June 1, 2019 Title - They Might Be Giants

ERINN

You're Lost Little Girl

Family Issues

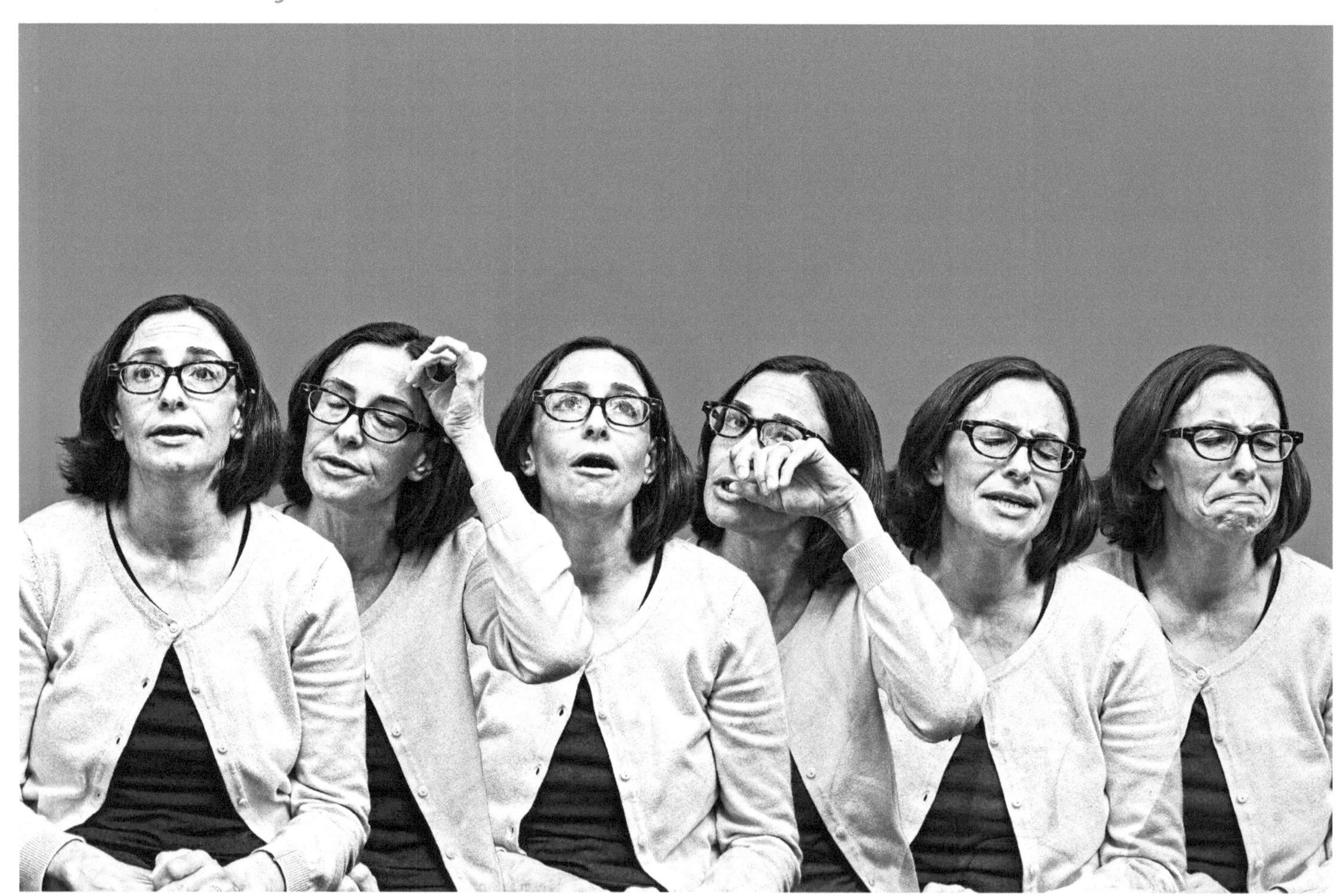

Story told on Thursday, May 17, 2018

Title - The Doors

AMANDA

Run For Your Life

Feeling Helpless, Witnessing Domestic Abuse

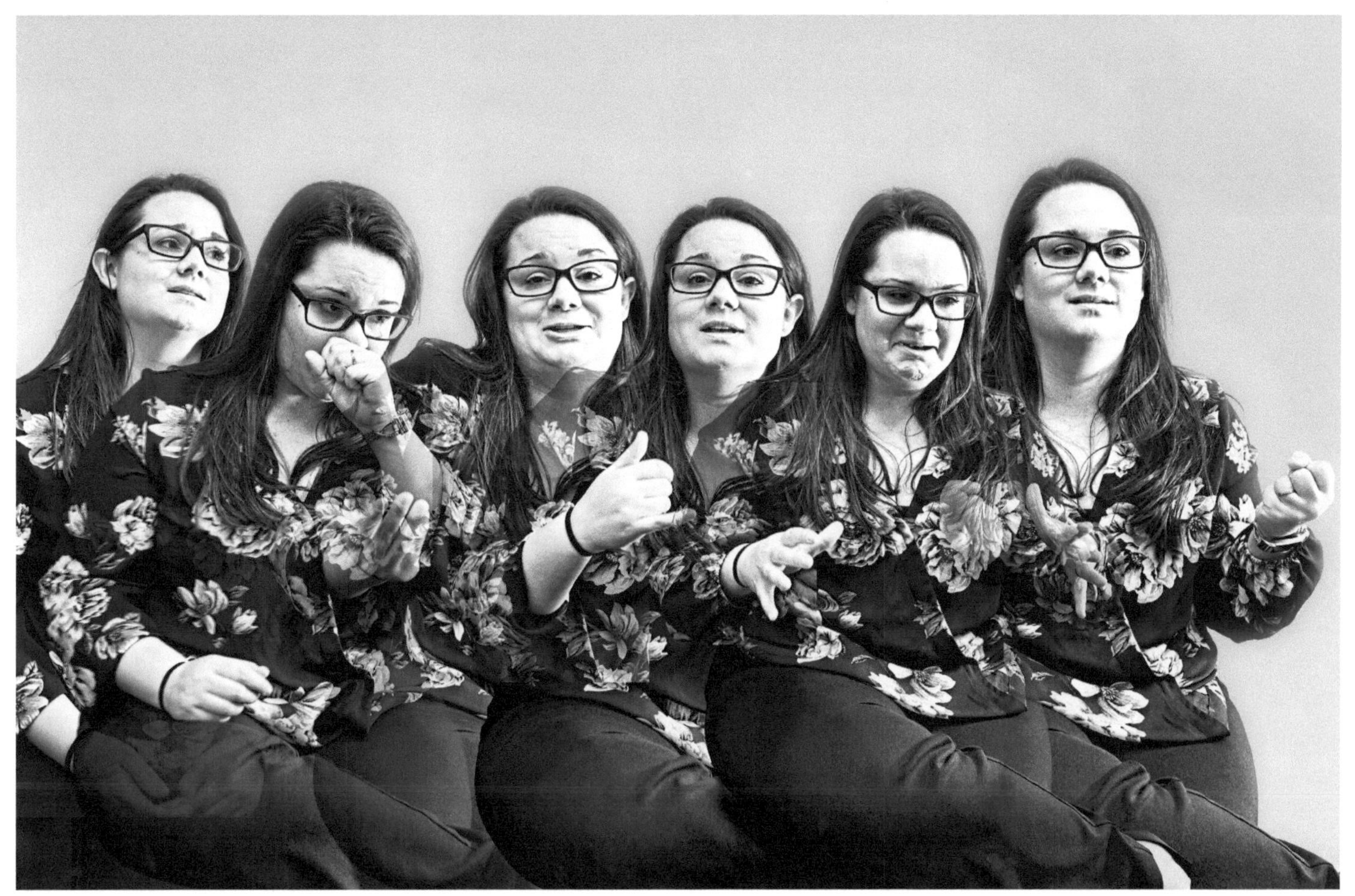

Story told on Thursday, April 11, 2019 Title - Lennon – McCartney

JEREMY

Under Pressure

Life Altering, Making Tough Decisions

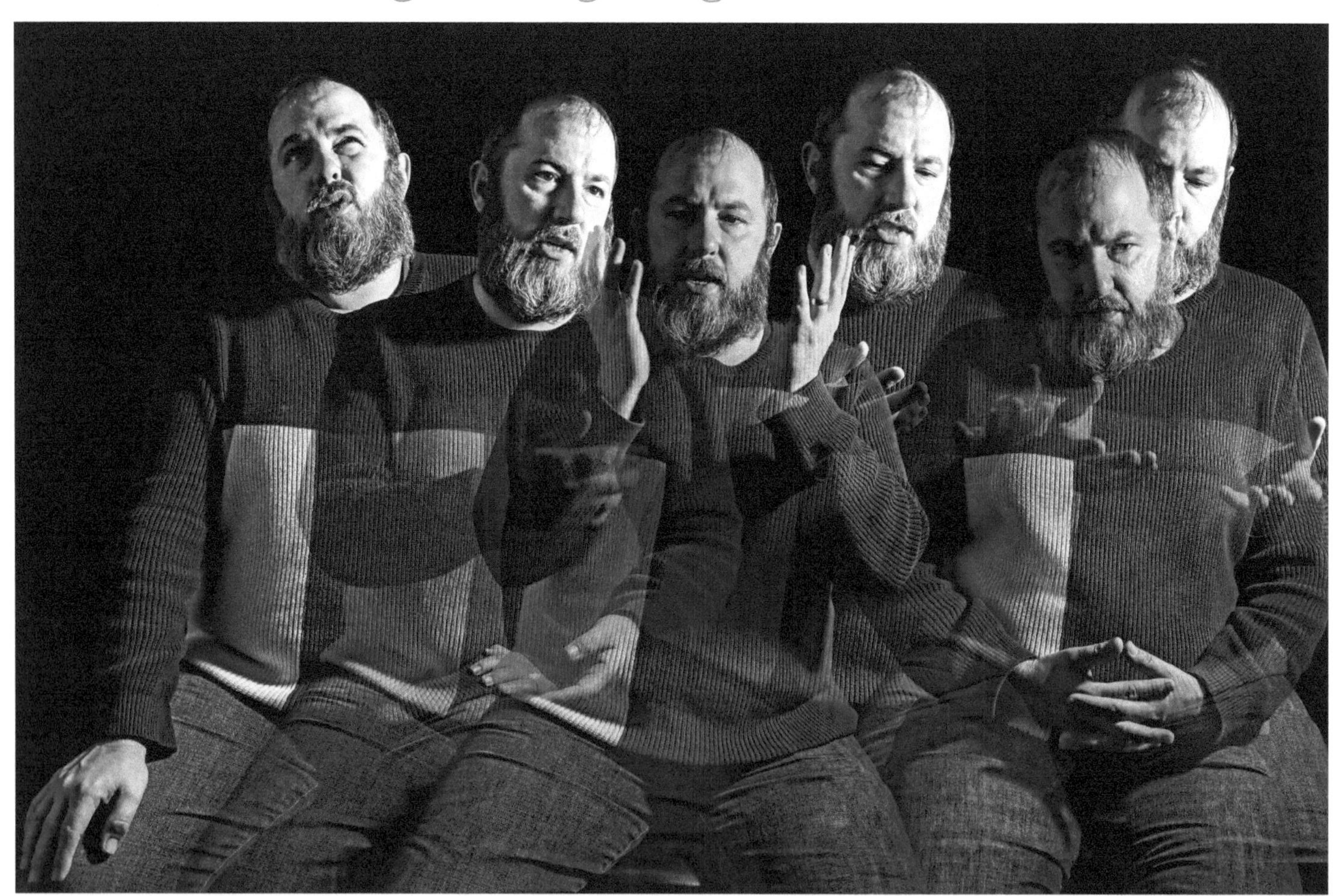

Story told on Monday, November 18, 2019 Title - Queen & David Bowie

TIM

Maggie's Farm

Job From Hell

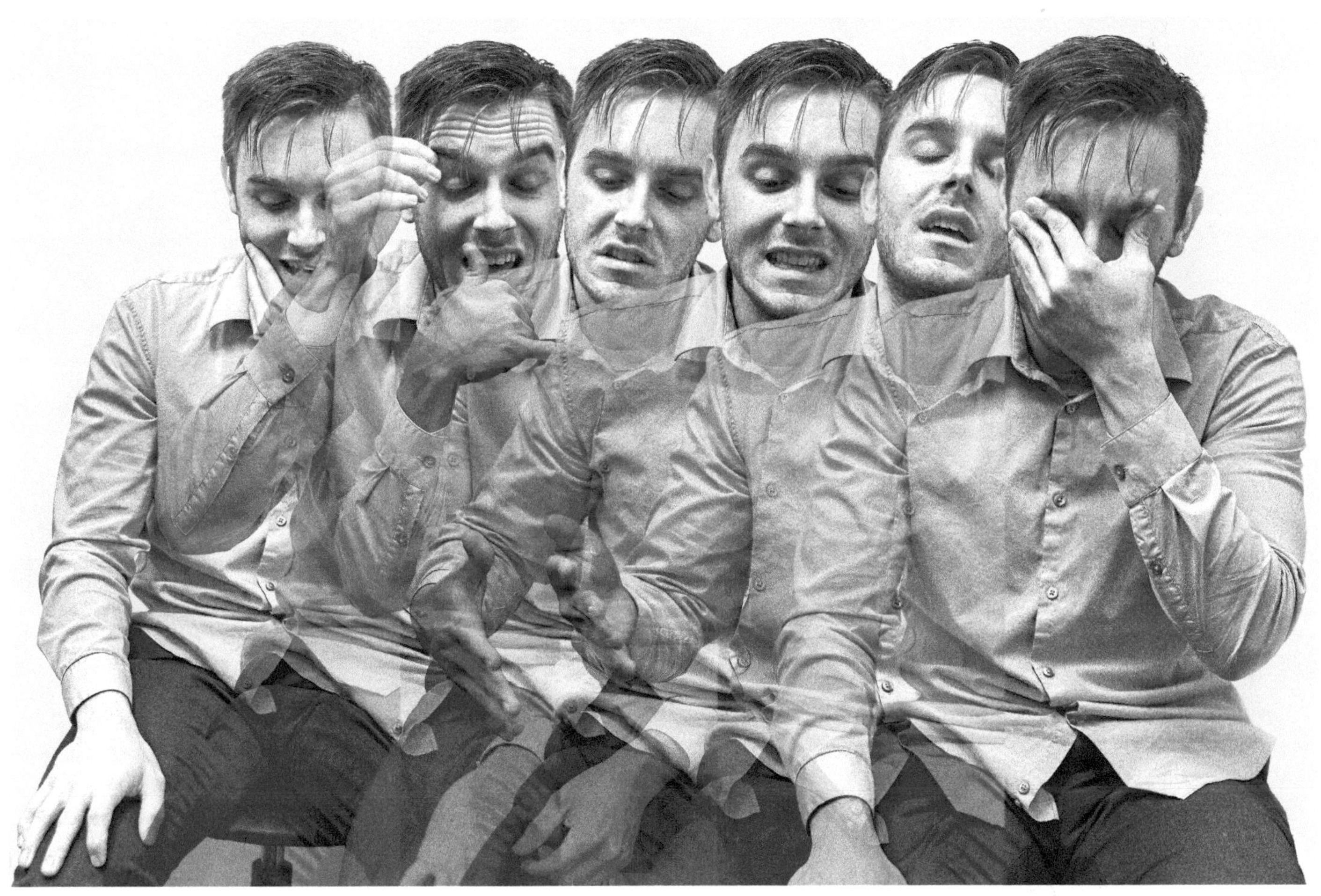

Story told on Thursday, March 29, 2018 Title - Bob Dylan

HEATHER

Here Comes The Sun

Joyous Expectations, Having a Baby

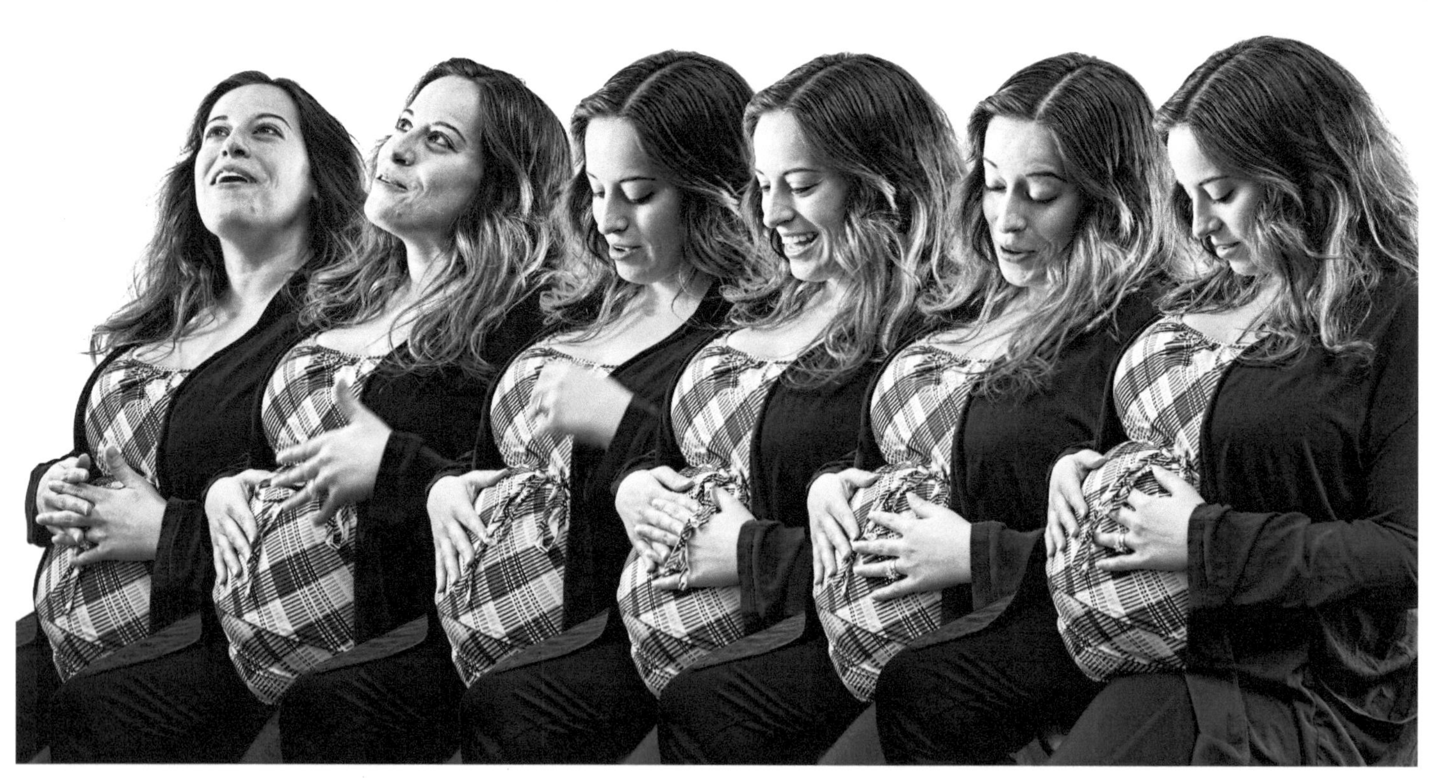

Story told on Friday, April 26, 2019

Title - George Harrison

SUE

One's On The Way

Hospital Visit for Him, Surprise for Us – "Should We Call a Cab?"

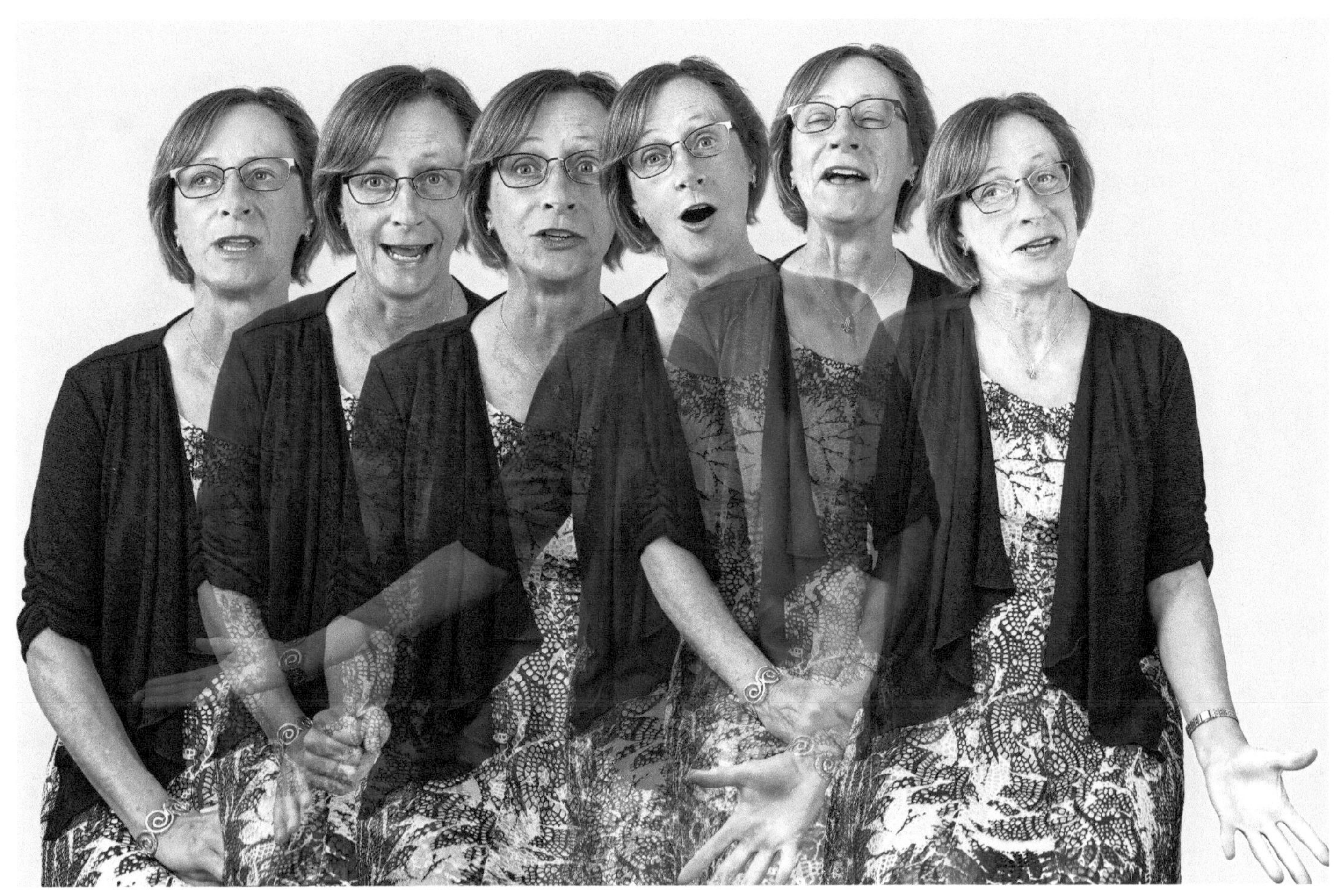

Story told on Saturday, September 21, 2019 Title - Loretta Lynn

CONNIE

Here Today

Remembrance, Family Loss Young and Old

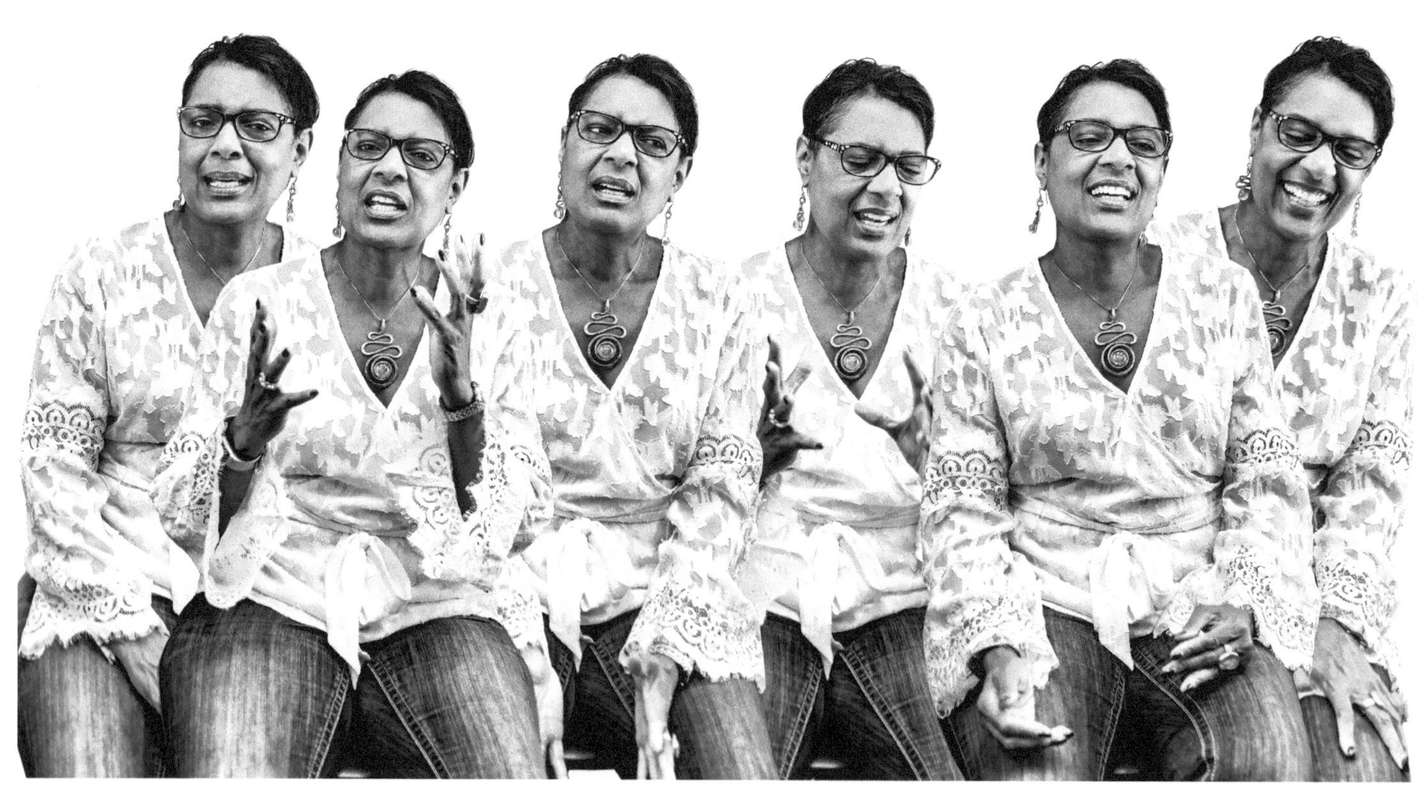

Story told on Tuesday, October 22, 2019

Title - Paul McCartney

JENNY

Tears In Heaven

Remembering Dad, He Never Saw My Baby

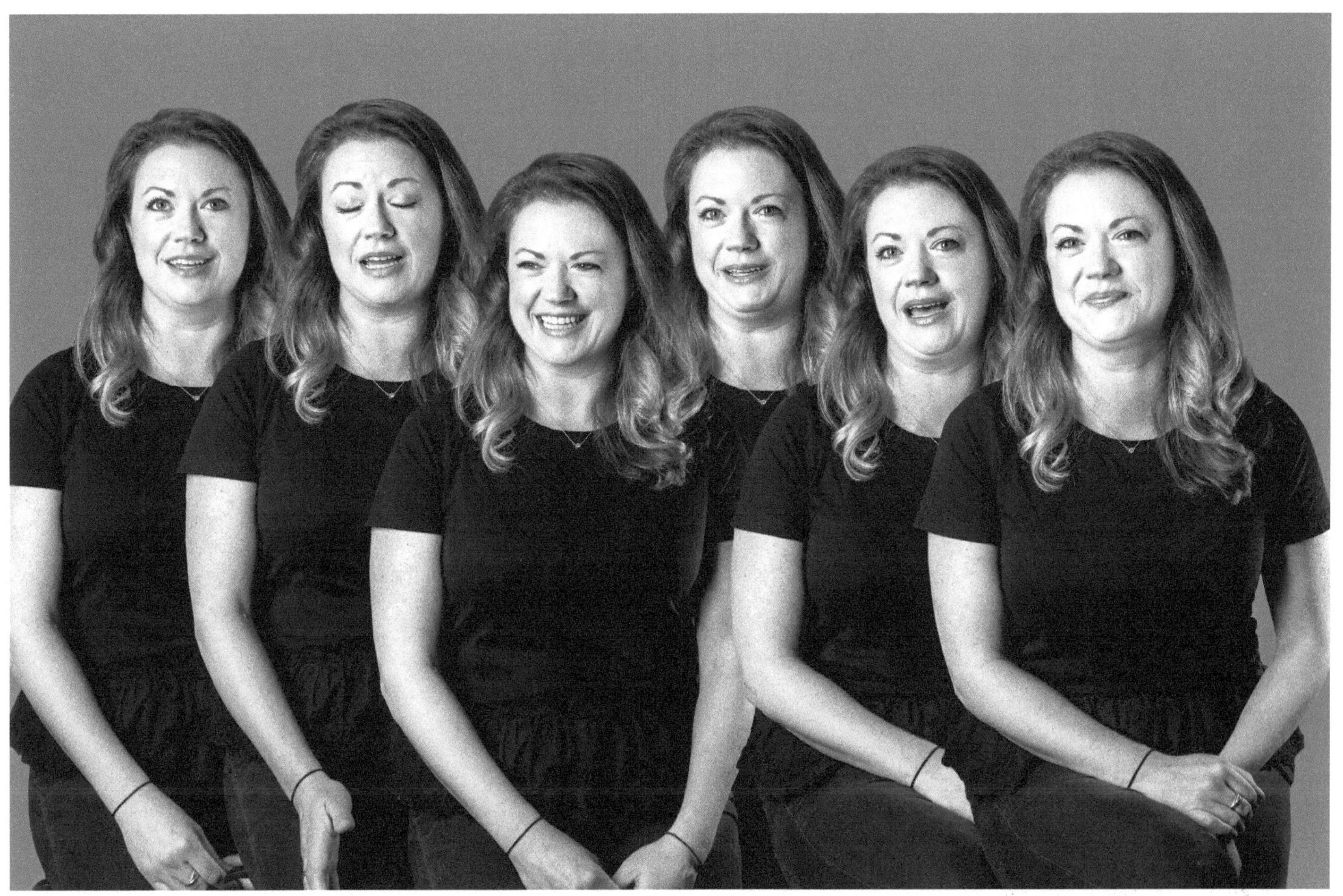

Story told on Sunday, September 15, 2019 Title - Eric Clapton

BEVERLY

I Love Paris

A Sensory Journey

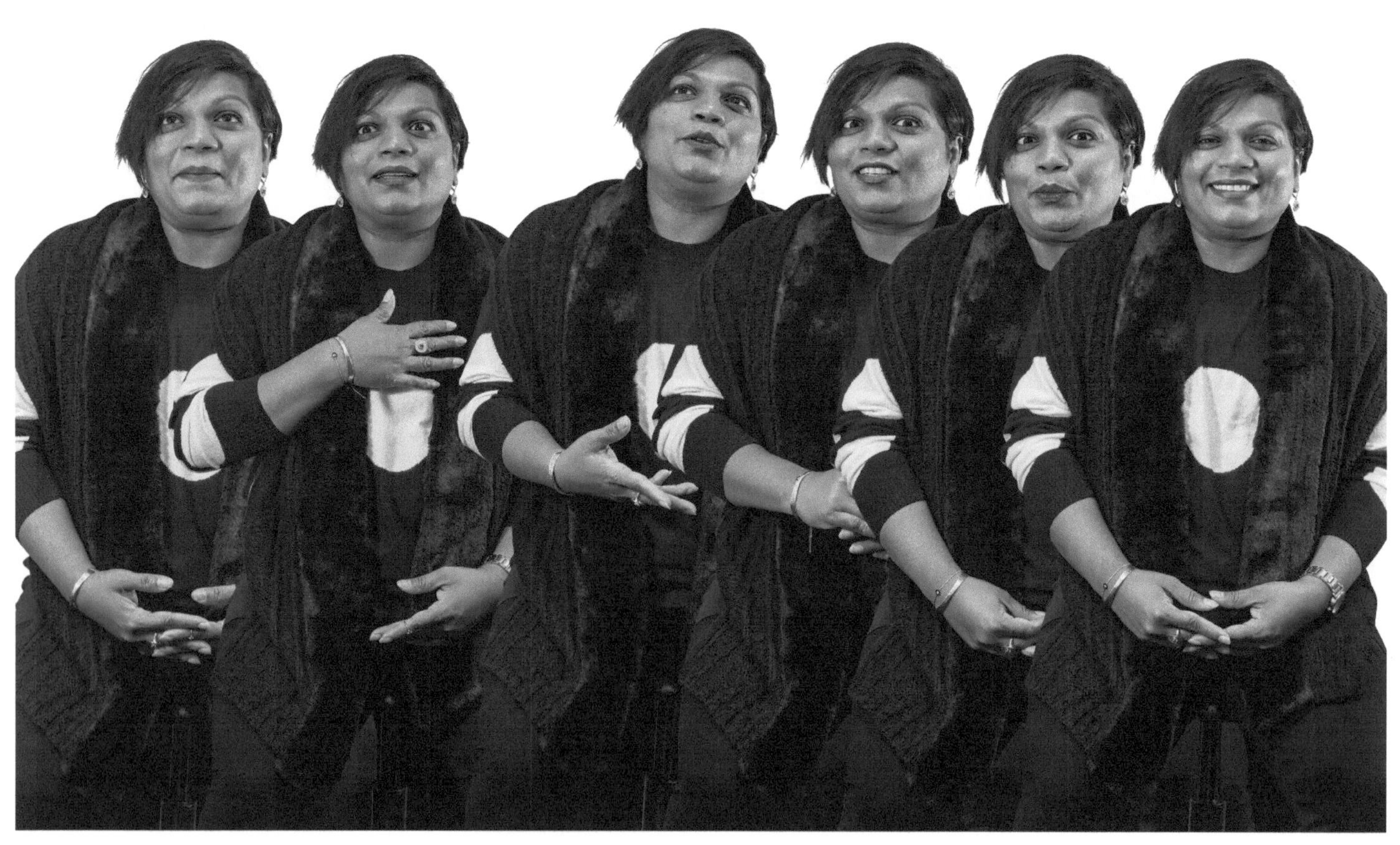

Story told on Tuesday, November 12, 2019 — Title - Cole Porter

AMANDA

Good Vibrations

How I Met My Husband; I Saw "Him" Standing There

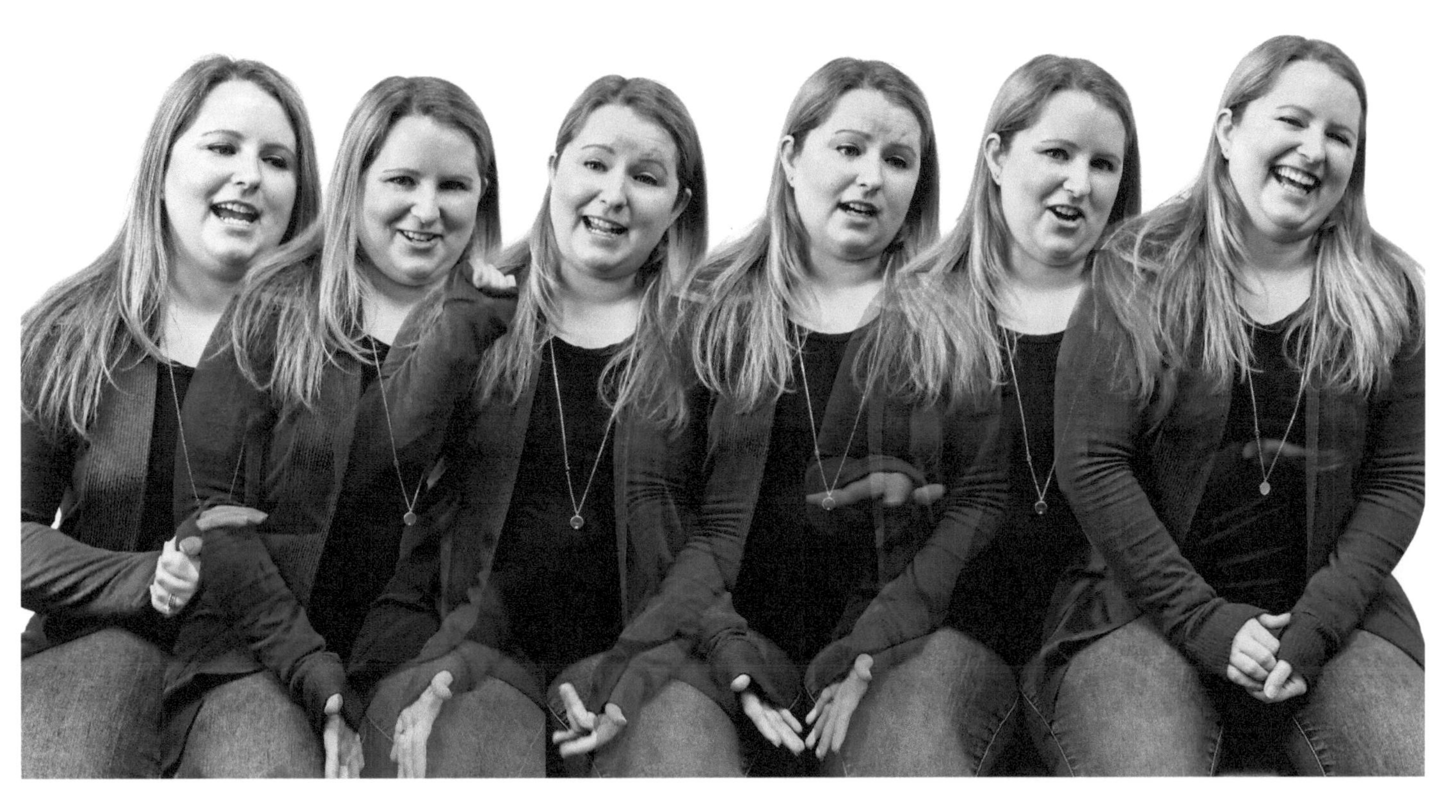

Story told on Friday, December 27, 2019

Title - Brian Wilson & Mike Love

ABOUT THE AUTHOR

NEAL SCHLOSBURG
in his own words

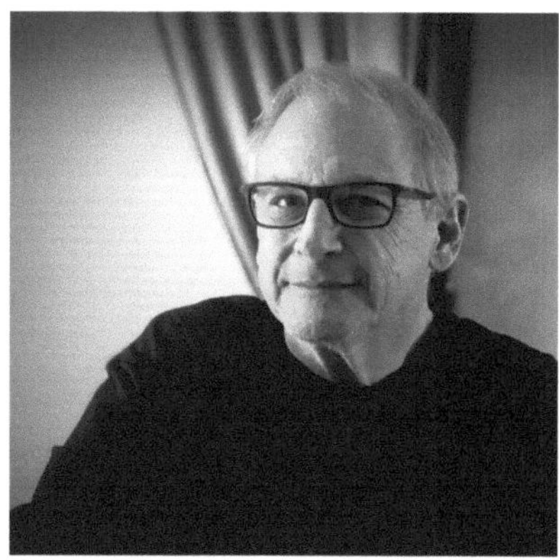

Music and photographs were the two passions that inspired my formative years. I first experienced photography through my father's family photos. I especially was intrigued with the development and outcome of images with the early Polaroid cameras. It's one thing to see the images when my father showed them to us, quite another to watch them develop.

My first involvement with photography wasn't with a camera; it was in a developing lab at summer camp. There was a darkroom where we made contact sheets. While that experience was limited, it was a springboard into a creative future.

My artistic creativity blossomed during my final two years of high school. In my family, voicing feelings was not welcomed, and certainly not encouraged. Through charcoal and pastels, I started to express my feelings. Looking back, my strongest expressions were in the form of sharp contrasts when using charcoal. The more complex ones seemed to emerge when I used pastels. There was something very cathartic about getting my fingers into the pastels as I blended and formed the textures and colors. At 19, not long after high school, my hands weren't as cooperative as they had been. It became difficult to continue using charcoal and pastels. I bought a camera.

During the time I progressed as a photographer, two major influences impacted me as an artist and my trust in sharing emotions. The first was a group of close friends that helped me believe it was safe to share my feelings without being judged. The second was my introduction to the work of Alfred Stieglitz. In the early 1900's, Stieglitz was one of the first, if not the first photographer to declare that photography was art. I was taken with his images of the human face, and to me, some of his photographs were reminiscent of works in charcoal.

Through those growth years, my interest in portrait photography evolved. Originally it was business portraits, but along the way I gravitated towards candid images of people. Along with Stieglitz, two other photographers influenced my work. The first was Herman Leonard, legendary jazz photographer. I loved the real time feelings that his images conveyed. I got the vibe of being right there in the room, front row center, watching, hearing, and feeling Dizzy Gillespie, Charlie Parker, Miles Davis, and many others create music magic. The other was brilliant photographer and author of this book's Forward, Jimi Giannatti. Jimi's iconic work on "Through These Eyes", portraits of seven iconic African American artists living and working in Los Angeles, gave me a window into their souls through his masterful lens art. The inspiration that these three photographers gave me are my artistic building blocks for *My Picture Tells A Story*.

Portrait Photograph by Julius Schlosburg.

I chose to not retouch my bio portrait. If the story tellers can show you who they are, so should I.

www.ingramcontent.com/pod-product-compliance
Lightning Source LLC
LaVergne TN
LVHW070155110826
845147LV00002B/411

* 9 7 8 0 5 7 8 6 3 6 7 6 4 *